Inlets *of the* Heart

LeRoy Payne Peach

UCCB Press

The University College of Cape Breton Press acknowledges the support received for its publishing program from the Canada Council's Block Grants program.

Cover design by Ryan Astle, Goose Lane Editions
Book design by Gail MacEachern
Printed and bound in Canada by City Printers, Sydney, NS.
Edited by Barbara Rendall

Acknowledgements: The cover is a watercolour, *The Blue Rocks of Lunenburg*, by Barbara Leewis (1983), in the collection of the author.

The pen and ink sketches are by Thelma Morrison (1997).

Canadian Cataloguing in Publication Data

Peach, LeRoy Payne.

   Inlets of the heart
   ISBN 0-920336-59-0

I. Title.
PS8581.E22I65 1998   C811'.54   C97-950235-7
PR9199.3.P 36165 1998

UCCB Press
Box 5300
Sydney, Nova Scotia
Canada B1P 6L2

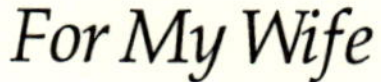

For My Wife

Contents:

The Circle Completed

Preface

In this, my third collection of poetry, I have described a journey in which "the wheel has come full circle"—from Morien Bay, Cape Breton to Toronto, and back again. It is journey in time and in spirit.

The first section of the book centres on early recollections of Cape Breton, with the birth of my remembering and the scraps of my forgetting. It is a Cape Breton that is insular, confined, pure, one that contains memories of my fisherman father and my mother, school, the fishing industry, recreation, culture. I live again what was precious and enduring.

In the second section, my Toronto years, I describe a sophisticated world of which, in my youth, I could only dream. It contains poems that deal with an urban landscape and an adopted culture. This section represents a moving out into a world that is complex, restless and acquisitive. To an extent, it is a world in which I feel like an exile, a world from which I eventually retreat.

In the final section of the book, I describe my return to the island and the changes that I see there. The wheel of memory and belonging comes full circle in that I am able to integrate into a culture which I left behind. I am once more in the loop, so to speak.

Many people have helped with this publication: Barbara Rendall, my excellent editor, who has made many helpful suggestions; Tom Rendall and Jan Curtis, both of whom read the manuscript and recommended it for publication; Gert MacIntyre, who made my work known to others; Beatrice MacNeil, who provided an outlet for my poetry through her reading ceilidhs; Penny Marshall, who guided me through the process of publishing; and finally my wife, who has heard my poems often and even suggested some of the lines.

A World Confined

"I have lost the key to the ancestral door."
"The Ancestral Door"

The Ancestral Door

Looking now at the faded coloured photo taken in '58 of you and me sitting on the living room couch, I think of a time when every word, every story, however often I heard it, was precious. Draped over the wine-coloured couch was one of Mom's white, starched doilies. I had my arm around your neck, my blue argyle ankle socks distracting. At twenty-five, I looked pensive, solemn, reverential, as though clinging to something that was leaving; you, serious, like a daguerrotype subject, your head full of eighty years of living, defying the camera to pluck out the secret of your seafaring soul. In your face, I saw power, I saw authority. It must have been Sunday. You had on your gray flannels, your best braces, your blue shirt, buttoned at the neck. You always asked me to button it for church, your gnarled fisherman's hands no longer doing what others took for granted. Your face was thin, making your nose even larger. How often you told me about your nose—how you were set upon by two men from Glace Bay while you were 'full'; how one had given you an uppercut, spreading your nose like a Negro's. Yes, you were a talker, a teller of tales: How you sang at the vaudeville concerts such popular numbers as 'The Old Tin Bucket That Hung On The Wall'...How you met Sir Charles Tupper once at a political rally...How you went one night to the Baptist Church and someone asked your friend if he was saved and your friend said, 'Go way, your breath smells'...How at election time in the early days, partisan supporters carried lead pipes to the telegraph office...How you went to sea in 1885, at the age of nine, got seasick daily, often vomiting blood...How before 1900 you only went to school in the winter and how the teacher gained his authority by beating the biggest bullies...How your father, who died at 91, took his toddy of rum each evening, smacking his lips in satisfaction...How your grandfather had his legs frozen at sea and amputated without the benefit of anaesthetic...And more, much more.

I wish today that I had asked you more, that I, like others, had understood that without the past we are diminished. Today I have the questions. Today I realize I lost more than a father of fourteen children, more than love, more than laughter. I have lost the key to the ancestral door, the substantial pageant behind the picture, the evidence behind the names.

Wharf Rat

I spent my school days
Amongst the fish heads,
The guts, the smell
Of cod liver oil
And the gluttony of gulls
At the local wharf,
Fishing and losing my shoes
Overboard and exploring
And dreaming,
Fascinated by the mysteries
Of swordfishing boats
From other ports.
Lingering late
Into the evening
'Til my mother dragged me
From the rigging
And I came like driven cattle
Up the lane with
A fishing rod in one hand
And a swordfish heart
In the other.
And then to bed
And up again in a maritime
Morning and into the sea
Before breakfast, the sea salt
Clinging like scales,
Then back to the wharf again,
My world so secure
And complete,
My dreams so confined
And so pure.

Setting Day

Debut of happy boats
Heaped with lobster traps—
Huge loaves of bread.
Blossom of buoys,
Beautiful freedom.
My father, my uncle
Happy as cats,
Content in the knowledge
That they had flung seeds
Into the faithful sea
Which had fallen on broken bottom
Would yield a harvest
Of red crustaceans.

Setting day:
The whole of Cape Breton
Entered the kingdom of hope
Through the door
Of an eternal labour.

For My Father

My father was a doer and a talker.
In six short months,
He rebuilt the local church.

After the green sea let him go,
When the waves' endless greeting
No longer filled his day,
He walked on his sea-legs
Up the lane and he rebuilt the church,
Burned down in a winter gale.
With their god-fearing hammers
He and his brothers
Pounded a way to glory,
Cast their nets on the land
And lo they harvested a spire,
Carved with love,
The focal point of living.

My father was a talker,
A teller of tales to God.
He got on his knees each night
An apparition in his white
Stanfield's underwear,
His bony knees on the
Cold linoleum floor,
And he prayed for half an hour,
While the rest of us
(And there were many)
Lay in our cosy beds
And mumbled meaningless words
Into the quilts
And drifted to dreams.

I see him now a figure
In white, ending his day
An ecological man—
His God, his church,
His brood, his sea
Woven within the fabric
Of his heart.

For My Mother

My motherly mother deep
Into kneading dough, turning
Experience into art, on her
Lips a Baptist hymn.

I turning experience into speech
Ask, "What do we have for lunch, Ma?"

Without altering her masterpiece,
Without looking up, she says,
"Oh-h...a little bit of everything."

As long as memory,
As long as bread is baked,
As long as hymns are sung,
I shall never forget her voice:
That "Oh."
That motherly inflection,
That blessing of faith and love.

Gowrie School: Grade Four

One time I said a poem.
Into the eyes
Of the King and Queen
Above the teacher's desk
I said it standing:
Of meadows and cattle
Silence and turning leaves.

It was autumn.

I was ten.

I lost that poem.
I never lost the feeling
Of that loss.

Older, I search through musty readers.
Older, even more, I want my poem back.

The Truth

Father was a voluble man.
Most mornings he held court
At the gray arborite table in the kitchen.
Would fold his eighty-year-old hands—
Knobbed and brown and liver-spotted—
Like an airtight argument,
Lean forward with
Some out-of-date advice for me.
His eyes were preachy, his face thin,
His nose prominent and veined.

The sea's chattel, he still rose early.
He would put on his tweed bill cap
And go down to the wharf,
Pretend he was going fishing,
And watch, like a reformed smoker
Who couldn't erase the appetite,
The locals leave for the lobster grounds,
Then chat up religion with the fish dealer.
He rarely used the street;
Instead, wharf-happy, he
Would climb the cliff,
Puffing like a spent jogger.

Often he'd take a set at me
About the superiority
Of the British.
Boy, the British
Can do everything.

But I was young and brash
And down from Dalhousie.
I had discovered things in books.
That the British had
The same clay feet as the rest of us
And I'd argue with my old father
To the point of rancour.
I'd get up and leave
And go down to the beach and meditate,
Watch the sea's intractability.

It was there in that wilful ebb and flow,
That chained melody,
That I learned a valuable lesson
I often failed to follow:
I wasn't about to change
My father's worldview
And he wasn't about to change mine, either.

Laughter

The time I heaved the baseball through
The garage window, I imagined the sound
Of shattering glass echoing throughout
The world, my father's rage to the point
That every time I saw him—in the yard,
At the wharf, in the lane—I ran the other way.
In those days there was a thing called
Discipline, a thing called authority.

So that when he came home that night
He asked my mother if she could explain
My bizarre behaviour. Told the reason,
He laughed uncontrollably.

I wish he were alive today so that
I could hear again that laughter,
See the crowfeet edges of his eyes
Crinkle—for he was a man of mirth.

But blessed is the memory. Blessed
Are those who no longer deal in voices
And yet can hear so keenly.

The Swordfish

Sunset, black spar, the homing boat,
Hopkins' little wharf.

Townspeople swarm like seagulls.

In the grave of the boat booted hunters
Stand amongst the silent warriors
Whose tapered swords are only
Ornamental now.

One black and silver behemoth
Hoisted on block and tackle hangs
Like a criminal, a black blood sucker
Trailing from its back, the dart wound
As fierce as sunset.

The fish is lowered, the pointed
Lower jaw aghast, the lustre of
The fixed black eyes protesting
The certain carving.

With long knives, experienced sea surgeons
Turn the fish belly-up, make
Careful incision from gills to anus.
Pull out guts like sofa stuffing,
Display them as booty, saving the
Massive liver, scraping the pink walls
Of the thick flanks, and cutting open
The stomach to look for souvenirs.
Half-digested herring sluice out.
They cut free the glistening red-sacked
Heart and white single valve like
A teat. Community wars have been fought
Over the heart, the drama extending

Right to the frying pan.
They weigh the gutted fish, the whole
Town waiting as at a boxing decison,
The verdict discussed for weeks.

And then the boat sails slowly
To its mooring, the people flying
To former perches.

Yes, in August, in Port Morien,
Swordfishing is everybody's business.

In The Days Of Rinks

On Big Pond,
We laced up under the lightpoles,
Our hands like stones, plunging
Warm feet into the wells of cold.
Happily the rink drew us into its
Oval white heart, warmed us under
The youth-approving moon. We wore
The pointed stars like cloaks,
Slithered along, swaying to
Imaginary music, the sound of our
Flashing skates like files on fish
Knives, our happy voices bouncing
Off the holy and impersonal night.

On Barro's rink,
Contendedly we froze our butts
Playing hockey in the open, on ice
Cracking with the cold, as the stringed
Lights waltzed to winter's tune.

At the Gowrie rink,
We stood like blissful snowmen
In the fierce frost, between periods
Warmed our hands before the pot-bellied
Stove, while returned servicemen
Fought in hand-to-hand combat the
Battle of Port Morien.

A little world then, focussed,
Forgiving. Nowadays, no rinks,
No outdoor skating. Layers and
Layers of different clothing.
In our living rooms, participatory
Mediocrity, informed sadness from
The man in the little square box.

We are wrapped and packaged,
Sophisticated—too damn sophisticated
For our own good.

Divine Intervention

In grade school I prayed from
The prayer book that I might pass
The examination. I arose early
On a sharp December morning and
I prayed in the kitchen before
The cosy coal stove. "We have erred
And strayed like lost sheep. We
Have left undone the things
That we ought to have done and
There is no health in us."

And I imagined the words of my mouth
Echoing in the fidgety sea fifty feet
From the kitchen window and the sea
Laughing derisively. Later, I trudged
To school, at each step the snow
Beneath my feet protesting my ignorance.
Neverthless, with God in the palm
Of my hand, I gave my scanty thoughts
To the skeptical foolscap before me.

Only today do I realize God's
Amusement at the little gaffer
In Grade Five pacing the room
At daybreak, putting his trust
In divine intervention.

Glace Bay, 1948

Every Saturday a shoot-up
At the Russell Theatre,
Roy Rogers the victor.

We came to town on the Morien bus,
Herbie or Speed at the wheel.
Twenty-five cents got you a seat
At the slaughter.

After the show, a hot turkey at Vihos
And back on the bus with the drunks
And home to our cosy beds.

Nowadays no communal Saturday nights,
The Russell lost to the slow decay
Of Commercial Street.

Nowadays crime in our living rooms
(With no discernible catharsis),
Our entertainment coat an imperfect fit
And much of our make-believe gone.

In The Days Of Trains

In the days of trains in the early '50s,
I left the Island for the Airforce,
My family seeing me off at Sydney.

Entering my berth, my brother
Asked me earnestly, "Can you tie
A Windsor knot?" as though
My whole world centred on neckties.

Landed in the alien world of St. John's, P.Q.,
Far from the shores of my insular island,
In the train station the jukebox playing
"I found my thrill on blueberry hill,"
With Uncle Louis Armstrong rasping out
The lyrics.

At the training base a corporal
Frightening me into obedience,
Threw me a broom and told me
To sweep the floor, I a naive Cape Bretoner
Who didn't know my ass from page nine.

In the days of trains I tortured
The language, speaking a Cape Bretonese
That only the gifted could translate
Imbued as it was with the culture
And singing landscape of the island.

Asked the man in the canteen once
For a pop called "Plus Four."
He said, "Where the hell are you from?"
I said, "They make it at MacKinley's in Glace Bay,"
Presuming, of course, that he knew the place.
"Where the hell is Glace Bay, fella?" he asked.
Yes, in the days of trains
I spoke with a broad brogue
About a world within a world.

Forty years later I'm back
On the mighty island, having been
Civilized in Toronto, trying
To tell it like it used to be.

My grammar got better. I ate
Lots of high culture, but my brogue,
Ah, yes, my brogue is still there, boy,
Cape Breton is still there.
No amount of Airforce or Hogtown
Could take the mighty island out of me.

Foxe Basin, N.W.T.: 1956

From my tent somewhere
Below the Arctic Circle,
I look out on a sameness.

The snow is yellowed,
Daily dim unyielding,
The frost a kind of stardust
On the parka. I am no hunter
In this hunting land,
Gather only my re-occurring
Thoughts, so many mental snowballs.

Here where the body bends
To a beautiful silence,
The babble of the world
Seems far away.

THEY'RE RIOTING IN AFRICA
The Arctic dawn's a muted blush today.
THE RUSSIANS CRUSH THE BRAVE HUNGARIANS.
The politics of snow is unencumbered.
THE TORIES CANCEL THE AVRO ARROW AIRPLANE.
The Caribou against a stark white morning
Admits no thought of loss.

In six months I return to Montreal
And sleep between the covers of white sheets.
Beauty and truth, simplicity and peace?
Ere long, before the days transform to spring,
After too many tragedies to count,
Or beers drunk at the seedier watering holes,
I soon bemoan events that do not matter,
Regard my Arctic interlude
As just a passing dream.

The Toronto Years

Hurting (Toronto, 1989)

At Harvey's, I order a hot dog,
With pickles, tomato, fries, Pepsi.

The washrooms are subterranean.
"The washrooms are unsafe," I say
To the manager. "What's to stop
A mugging? There are people out there
With no money, people hurting."

"People with money hurt, too," he says.

From a wall speaker, a woman sings
In a plaintive voice, "I fall to pieces...."
At the next table, two students discuss
The state of the world. "Things are
Falling apart; nothing can be done,"
He insists. "No, nothing can be done,"
She says.

I am surprised by the paper taste
Of the fresh frozen fries. I am
Surprised by the taste of the hurting.

Massey Hall: 1981

At the symphony, the Russian pianist
Jousted with the Japanese conductor—
The winner, Camille Saint-Saens.
The ample lady galloped, whilst
The maestro, like a toy soldier,
Stood his ground.

As sure as a tigress attacking
She pounced on the bass and
Followed with flaming cadenza
And wild salterello. Black-clad,
The conductor then countered
With slashes and probes. The
Audience reeled with respect.

Sound floated to century-old
Ceiling, the wooden seats of
The second balcony. I wanted
To bottle it up and let it out
At the door of the world, in the
Heart of commercial heaven,
Near the record shops, the punk
Rock, the muzak, the cut-rate
Albums, the strip joints,
The hard-sell clothing stores,
The babble of tongues from the
Clubs.

But realistically, I left the art
At the dying building and walked
Up the sufficient sidewalk past
An army of sufficient people to
The subway system and kept
My music to myself.

Rituals

My wife's get-up stretch
Signals my lying in.
She carries my
"Make-me-a-nice-breakfast"
Into the kitchen, runs water,
Turns on sports, makes coffee,
Porridge, toast. "Your breakfast's
On the table."

I uncoil, define our roles
By asking, "Where's my orange?"
My wife, who could have said,
"Would you like to wear it?"
Says, "Of course, your orange."

Seated to the CBC, I'm missing
Peanut butter, dare not get up
To get it, fearing confusion
Of roles. My wife perceives it
Missing, does not move.

And then the sports: my Leafs
Have lost again. My wife,
Remembering the orange, says,
"The circus continues."

Despite her cutting comment
And her laughter, ritualistically,
I rise, pour both of us a coffee
And, yes, I get the peanut butter too.

Love I

From my condominium
Overlooking the municipal golf course,
I see grown men,
Motley against the green,
Bag-packing hikers, with strides
As wide as scissors opening and
Closing—grown men, with weapons
Flashing silver on daylight, boxing
The ears of a little white ball
That howls to the greener green,
Then patting it lovingly on the head
And sending it hopefully into Australia.

No man hath greater love than this:
That he would give up family
Every weekend for his "friends."

Love II

In single file, one father first,
Four goslings, last one mother,
The goslings in a moving prison
Of love.

This road troupe green and golden
Crosses the path of an avid golfer,
Moving prisoner of love.

Without any indication that they
Understand the complexity of
This addiction—the programmed
March to par, reverence of
Relationship, alignment, address,
Tented concentration, babied clubs,
The exact amount of spin imparted
To the sphere—with arrogant
Indifference to these things,
The geese, one honk chasing the
Other, over a gosling silence,
March on, and in their 'strut
and fret' act as the only lovers
In the world.

Toronto Highrise

Elevator opens,
Swallows man
And child and me.

I nod.
The other
Mumbles.

The baby smiles,
An act of grace
That washes over us.

Elevator opens,
Admits a young girl glum.

The baby smiles.

I now am newly happy,
The glum, suspicious girl
Restored to health.

Elevator empties
Girl and me
And man and beatific one
Into the serious world.

Walking to underground
I thank the Lord
For small things smiling.

Of A Dog Walking His Mistress

O lady blonde alone,
Each day I see your little blonde dog
Tugging you along the avenue.
His is the face of perfect adoration;
Yours is the face of duty.

I see you walking together,
He forcing you to participate
In the territorial imperative,
To do what's best for him,
To make him feel important.

Soon you will carry your world
Into the condominium,
Until the evening awakens
And the ritual begins again.

A Lady Takes The Sun

Below my balcony a lady takes the sun.
She prances out as if she were on stage,
All poses and angularity.
Unfolds a blue cot, produces a white cap,
Takes off her shift and shows a tight bikini,
Plasters herself with lotion,
Adjusts her bra, rubs her waist,
Around her breasts, along the sides of legs
And then her feet.

She puts dark glasses on,
And like a flower
Opens her petals
To Sol.

Preparation time ten minutes;
Frying time two hours.

Is it for me she makes this vanity?
I speculate the badge of summer
Is rarely worn for no-one.

Hey good lookin', what's cookin'?

With a sixth sense
She rises, adjusts her bra,
Covers herself with a towel,
And looks up to the twenty-first floor.

Suddenly I am merely a middle-aged man
Leaning over a balcony, fantasizing
About a young woman
Who seeks only her privacy.
From the kitchen
The smell of bacon and eggs.

I imagine us at at dinner.
Candlelight and roses
Moonlight and poses.

Must I go on like this?
Imagination is the greater bliss.

Dining In Old Quebec

In old Quebec
On an evening in August,
With wind retired,
The weary sun
In nightclothes,
I watch the wordless
Diners walk possessed
To evening food
Like worshipers
Who stream
To mid-day mass.

Once in,
Their dining
Is a sacrifice.
Every mastication,
Even their minor gestures,
Part of a higher,
Deeper ritual.

This is to celebrate
That world
That never can be
Ordered into words.

The Pope In Toronto: 1984

A press of people.
The Pope arrives
In a bullet-proof bubble.

The Pope descends.

Polite applause.

A beatific smile.
A face as true as spirit.

Christ's sword-bearer
Living a guarded life.

Some people want to
Place him on a cross.

Such is the march of progress.

On Finding My Book In A Second-hand Bookstore

I'm on a ladder
Leading to the heights of creativity,
Overwhelmed by the inexhaustible word,
Looking for Pratt's poetry.

Peeking out at me
Is Peach's *Heartreign*.

I do a double-take.
Pratt and me together?

We never know
Where brainchildren will go
When we release them
To a breathless world.

Autumn Leaves

I never look at autumn leaves
Without a new humility.
Their rage,
Their anarchy,
Their last-ditch stand,
Futile though it may be,
Teaches unyielding glory,
Tells me, in fact,
That each day's journey
Should blaze with a similar beauty,
A similar truth.

Of A Lady Drinking Coffee At
A Traffic Light In Spring

"Restless, restless were the gods and always in motion."
By The Waters Of Babylon

See the young lady at a light,
Her chalice lifted to the Age,
As she observes her coffee rite,
Frenetic on a public stage.

The light turns green; she crawls ahead
And enters in the traffic's flow
With some dexterity, some dread
Until she gains the stop-and-go.

The stop-and-go goes on and on
A linkless chain in morning's rush,
A moving prison; no antiphon
To nature's beauty, nature's hush.

O daughter of Machine and Time,
O modern worker on the run,
The buds, the clouds are still sublime
E'en though you dwell in Babylon.

Religion, Florida-style

The flat white sand, a marble floor,
Holds in the heat haze the tangle of legs
As far as the eye can see.

Worshippers not standing bake
In the severe sun to alligator brown,
Like alligators in a phony sleep—
Burnt offerings in the silicon
Of their salvation.

Here the sea, the indifferent deity,
Jelly-rolls in, collapses, retreats
Before the lotion-covered charismatics—
Lying, reclining, standing, sauntering,
Baking, re-baking—creating
The masks they will flaunt
Among winter's anemics.

This is the land of no regret
Where to worship
Is to tan,
To tan is to live!

Driving Up Kissimmee Boulevard

I'm driving up Kissimmee Boulevard
In West Palm Beach, after consuming
A bottle of wine and a plate of shrimp,
My wife in the front seat,
My mother-in-law bringing up the rear.

By my speed, I am brushing back
The darkness.

In the rear-view mirror,
I see blue lights flashing.
Is there an ambulance?

I pull over.

A man gloved and helmeted,
A motor-cycle man, a cop
Approaches, his gun drawn.
He keeps well to the rear.

Did you-all see them blue lahts?
Yes, officer I saw the blue lights.
Do you-all know what them blue
Lahts stand for?
In Canada we use them on ambulances.
He is livid at my unintentional
Cheekiness.
Don't be funny, mistah. You-all from Canada?
Yes, sir, I say, having already told him.
How long you-all here for?
I leave tomorrow, I lie.
Well, I got a gud notion to give you
A sahtation. Now you-all obey
The speed limit, you hear?
You Canadians act as if you-all
Own this State...
Escaping the citation,
(In Canada a traffic ticket),

We pull away as though in a
Funeral procession, my wife
Hardly containing herself.
Shook up but relieved, I laugh
The laughter of the close call.

On the way back to Canada,
Where cop cars wear red,
We travel to the black hills
Of Tennessee,
The bluegrass country of Kentucky,
The desolation of Ohio.

I watch my speed.

Recalling suddenly the encounter
With the Palm Beach policeman,
I yell out mockingly,
"Ah got a gud notion to give you
A sahtation."

My mother-in-law pipes up:
"You weren't laughing that night,
Buster. You were pretty scared
That night."

Mothers-in-law have a way
Of stifling laughter.

Commencement At Nowhere High School

At Nowhere High School's commencement,
The V.P. emceed the evening.
A slight man, a United Church minister,
Gave the invocation. Attributed to God
The hard-earned marks. And then
The school board member, a man
Whose specialty was wire fences,
Got in the act. Nowhere was wonderful, he said—
"Super" students, "super" staff,
Quality next to none.
The V.P., short in every way, praised
The gentleman's perspicacity—in fine,
His 'sage' remarks.
Obsequiousness personified,
The principal then heaped praise on praise.
He said that Nowhere was a growing woman
Well endowed—a most unfeeling gaffe.

And then things fell apart:
The male announcer acted
As though he were drunk.
The valedictorian's words were cliché-ridden.
Some students came in shorts;
Others began to editorialize.

After the ceremony, the principal
Claimed the conduct was untypical.

But staff who had been there for years
Declared that they could tell a peach
From a lemon.

October Snow

Before the red leaves' leaving
White winter snow came
Stealthily by night.

By day (a sun day) we had
Ice-cream heaped on glazed
Strawberries, meringue on lemon.
We ate it with our eyes.

By evening the topping was all gone,
Leaving the strawberries,
The lemon, the longing.

Yet gratefully, on the unimaginative
Freeway fighting our way forward
The unassailable after-image, too.

Examination

Outside,
Winter's script:
Slanting snow
Is perfect
For the month,
Deserves A-plus.

Within,
White-outs:
Thirty-two pupils
Snowing on *Romeo and Juliet*
In a swirl of misconception.

Examiner
Sits smilingly
In the storm.

Romeo and Juliet
Entombed.

A real snowjob.

For Those In The Trenches

Teaching the story
"Odour of Chrysanthemums"
So that I was certain that students
Could smell the regret, could see
That the flowers fading to the colour of tea
Signified that the marriage had drifted
Into the shallows of recrimination,
I glanced to the back of the room
Where Wesley Smith was sleeping,
His girlfriend, in a dream of endless love,
Watching the clock.

D.H. Lawrence had had me
In a bearhug of resignation:
I was lost, lost in the sadness the heart felt
When the head decided everything was ended.

Too lost to see that for so many people,
Art's agony is nothing but a snore.

Poetry Workshop

In a portable squat, freezing,
We find ourselves combining words
Into profundity.
Words refuse our bidding
Will not blend. The will says:
"Words, come forth!"
Imagination, insolent, replies:
"Poetry has no commerce
With the will."

The morning is prosaic.
We feel embarassed. How could we
Possibly explain the absence
Of inspiration? We came in faith
Over the spring-brown fields
Stretching from white sleep
And all we do is rustle
Blue-lined paper.

A custodian appears,
Turns up the thermostat.
But, oh, I am so sad to say
Poetic thoughts
Do not respond to heat.

For Langston Hughes

I ate today your morsel
Of immortality on dreams
That drift and dissipate
Like wake waves.
Tasted a wonder.

Can you now give me some
Advice about coming to terms
With reality?

I look at the sky
(Shakespeare's great canopy),
Hear of holes in the ozone layer,
Foodbanks, homeless youth in
Downtown Toronto.

When dreams die, we have
A broken-winged society.

They say two poems equal
One valium, make palatable
Many realities.

Can you give me another poem?

On Seeing The Play
"Romeo and Juliet" at Stratford

The yellow bus crawled through a
Countryside turning tail on summer,
Past the I-told-you-so trees,
By the terminal smiles of marigolds,
Fortune's fools, trusting fields,
Billboarded with end-time messages:
"Prepare to meet your maker...."
"Jesus is coming."

Even the patient cattle sensed
That the drama would end in death,
The antagonist autumn, 'beautiful tyrant,'
Winning.

We came into the playhouse reverently
And spilled around the open, solemn stage
With lovers' balcony and jutting truth.

The star-crossed lovers entered;
We became them. Saw them
Turn tail on hatred, flouting fortune,
Invent a thousand ways to hoodwink adults,
Wept, too, when they were weeping.
Died when they died.

At dusk we surfaced from the dusky tomb
And lumbered through the autumn-chastened land,
Chastened by love. Pity and fear
Had fled, and we were calm,
Calm as the cornstalks,
Changed as the changing trees.
For we had travelled far
Into the land of faith
And self-deception.

My Cardinal

My cardinal called at noon.

I was sitting on my balcony
Looking for beauty
In examinations.

That worthy came,
Alighted on a fence
And cut the city-sound
With happy song.

No answers
Sang
As gracefully
As he.

For Barfield And Baseball: 1983

The centre field bleachers,
The enormous Sunday crowd
Of laid-back believers.

A ball lofted by the bat
Of Jesse Barfield
Soars ever so slowly
Hanging and turning and
Gathering the afternoon sun.

As certain as Sunday
A homer.

The ball arcs
Over the wire fence.
The crowd rises
In ecstasy.

One fan naked
Except for shorts
Catches the manna
Barehanded.

O heavenly sphere!
O transformed fan!
O blessed Barfield!
O Baseball!
I have entered
Your kingdom
Forever.

Heaven And Hell In The NHL

Coming into the subway
In the slow sweep
Of a crushed and happy crowd,
The Leafs having broken
Their fifteen-game losing streak,
I saw a big man standing
At the entrance holding up a sign
With sayings: "Ye must be born again...."
"For God so loved the world...."
And doing Christianity a disservice
By preaching a steady stream
Of patent nonsense, such as,
"You are now in hell...."
"You like hockey, you'll never go
To heaven...." "The devil wants you
To like hockey to take your mind
Offa heaven...."

But in truth
I had just come out of hell
And I *was* in heaven.
I was born again, boy.

No amount of preaching
Could convince me
That Jesus wasn't happy for me.

Seagulls And Sunday Golfers

On that magnificent Sunday morning,
I remember kneeling, making each putt
A prayer, walking, making each walk
A pilgrimage, then looking up and
Seeing the gulls again, a shifting
Tableau on blue, a wounded chorus
Circling and intersecting and drifting
In a slow and dreamy daze.

And I and my friends imprisoned
By belief, obsessed with parabolic
Flights and flagsticks.

Truly, I wanted to break out
And reclaim the earth and sky.
But the man said, "It's your turn
To putt now...." And all of a sudden
The doors were locked, and I was
Back in my cell again, with all
The shades pulled down.

Progress

Farms die beneath cement,
Stocks dwindle in the sea.
The pristine sky, I must lament,
Is smudged by you and me.

Yet still man's beat goes on
Oblivious of fears.
The battered universe unfolds
And sheds its acid tears.

Down, down a-down we go
And singing all the way.
Upon the slippery slope we sing
The brave millennial lay.

Social History: 1980

Birds
Like drunks at a sing-song
Herald the dawn.

I wake:
The shower faucets opera.

I drive:
The freeway hums a mantra.

I work:
Where are the melodies here?

"Sphinx In Danger Of Losing Shoulder"

For Percy Bysshe Shelley

We know that the Egyptian Sphinx—
In ancient art none bolder—
Is subject to the finite jinx:
Has lost a bit of shoulder.

That desert flowering of art,
That Gizeh man and lion,
That monument of love and heart
Is now a faded shrine.

Nature and time conspired to pit
And ridge its famous face.
It took a recent storm to split
Its body near the base.

Some think that we should feel the pain
Of its slow, sure demise,
But we still have the desert reign,
The constant changing skies.

The Almost Meeting

At dusk through the leaves
Of the spring-coiffed beech,
Each leaf defined against
A sleepy sky, I search
For the bringer of song.

In beech's labyrinth
Cardinal concert.

And I whirling under
The serenaded sky
To catch a glimpse
Of that scarlet elusive truth,
Heart in my mouth
Through melody.

He shifts his ground and sings.
I shift my ground and search
But never see him.

Tired of the intrusion,
He darts away, his singing
Bouncing off a nearby river.

And I there feeling foolish,
Rejected by time and beauty,
Looking now through less defined leaves
Into a sleep-filled sky.

Sonnet (1985)

In sacred dawn when all the world is true,
The sunrise pulls the jagged curtain back,
Gives us the headlands; then a boat or two
Sails into bronze, is silhouetted black.
Gulls whine and wake me happy for that song
And I am one with all I hear and see.
Even the scheming crows that meet and throng
Add meaning to this sharp reality.
The gold outside my window, in this hour
I contemplate the symbols I have known:
Apartment building, freeway, monied tower,
And waking early to the traffic's drone.
In incremental daylight I decry
All that has kept me from my sea, my sky.

Down Home: 1977

Before I close my eyes forever,
I want to sit daily on my sun deck
And look at Morien Bay,
That famous king,
His diadem two headlands,
His only jewel Flint Island.

I want to watch South Head,
The smiling snake,
Where my great-grandfather settled,
After he left Sydney, and then
The beetle-browed Cape Perce
Brooding over the entrance
To Morien Harbour.

I want to see the sea's beautiful anger cool,
The bay rock itself to sleep.
I want to see the red light of the bell buoy
Beating its evening rhythm on the oily
Calm water.

Before I close my eyes forever,
I want to walk the changing beach,
Wade out to the Big Reef
And tantalize the crocodile sea.

I want to pick blueberries at Blockhouse
Holding them lovingly
Between thumb and forefinger
And hearing them plop in the pail.

I want to sit on the wharf
And meditate and plan
And lift big smelts
From the cool November water.

Before I close my eyes forever
I want to love the land to pieces.

I want to thank God I am home at last.

Down Home: 1978

Late summer.
There is the harbour:
Gulls sitting placidly awaiting
Fishing boats that never come;
Boats pinned to wharf by
Inconsiderate winds; cormorants,
Suspicious as groundhogs, sitting
On lobster crates; wind sending
Black swords of water over the dock
Like darting fish.

There is the bay:
Benevolent dictator, beautiful god,
Shrouded in one place by those
Inky rain clouds, star-showered
Elsewhere. Headlands embrace it.
And island greets, guards.

The town:
A technicolour town, each house
A fist, held in defiance
To a testy sea. I walk its
Different streets a stranger here,
Seeking the pathways back to
Former days. A coasting hill has
Now become a road, holding no more
The laughter, joyful voices—
The poetry of childhood.

Where is the well-trod lane?
Oh, how we cherished it when life
Was nothing more than imagination,
The future a treacherous ocean
We did not think to travel.

The school yard overgrown with weeds?
The school torn down?
I see us now as little soldiers

Mustered from playing fields
And from the constant woods,
The buck-toothed master tolling
The death of summer, the waning
Of our days.

The skating pond so huge in former times
Carries today no traces of romance,
Nor longing for romance.

As well, there was a time when
I could name the people walking,
Their houses by the colour and design.
Those are all gone; those landmarks
Aren't the same.

Late summer.

We cannot deny what we have known,
Nor can we fully accept the things that are.

The Return

I'm counting the days to Cape Breton
When I'll travel the road to my land.
I'll leave behind all of the fretting
And drive to a peace that is grand.

For a village that borders an ocean
As timeless as tide's ebb and flow,
Inspires in me sweet devotion
And gives my heart reason to glow.

I grew in this beautiful landscape;
Like so many I left it behind.
But the culture I knew I could never escape;
Yes, the ties that have formed me still bind.

There's the sea and the sense of belonging,
A security money can't make.
There's the land, a perpetual dawning
And the magic of every daybreak.

There's the people as tough as the coastline
With a humour to laugh off their pain,
A togetherness seamless as skyline
And an inner resource of disdain.

I'm counting the days to Cape Breton
When I'll travel the road to my land.
I'll leave behind all of the fretting
And drive to a peace that is grand.

The Circle Completed

"The wheel is come full circle."
King Lear

Schooner Pond

Autumn storms attract me to this place,
A godforsaken cove where father fished,
Where northwest winds
Bullied the sea and shore.

And so in this November storm
I park my car upon a jut of land
Right before the lot where father
Had his fishing Shack and boathouse.
It is as close as I will come to history,
Though not as close as I have come to him.

Waves plume and fall apart
Like a bad argument.
Surfing gulls slide peacefully between
Troughs as though the storm
Had wakened in them
Some primeval worship.
A brown kelp heaps upon the sand.
A net of buntings flings away to forest.
And at a nearby headland
Surf flounces like a Spanish dancer
Against cliffs that die daily.

Like Lear I stand before the howling wind
Calling up dated memories:

Make-and-break engines
Drumming the sacred dawn.
Boats playing hide and seek
In coastal swells.
My father's voice,
Imperious, excited at landfall,
His pipe clenched firmly in his mouth,
His sons like dead men in the boat,
Green around the gills from dirty weather.
The fishing fleet laid up on slips like trout,
The gritty fishers placing the crates of lobsters
Into the dealer's truck.

I see an unpainted Shack
Where father and his brothers
Lived on weekdays—
Half-eaten homemade bread
Lying upon the stark linoleum table,
The smell of disorder,
Clothes scattered on chairs,
Oilskins in the porch,
The rank reminders of a dubious trade.

And I can hear the crackling argument,
Its certain dissipation into a night
Of song and rum-drenched laughter.

These are all attestations of a spirit.
They are the scraps I've drawn
From my forgetting.

November storms attract me to this place,
A clean slate now,
Empty of everything
But mocking laughter.

In Winter: Port Morien, 1990

The long headland
In a black and white sleep.

Geometry of ocean:
Plane, plenitude, palpable, aloof,
Holding me in the palm of its hand
Never embracing me.

I have grown old enough
To accept personal impersonality,
Content only to watch the planed sea,
Its blue-starch slob ice
Or larger floes themselves—
Convoys in a sinister silence.

Each day a stark renewal:
Land white-wonderful,
Sea awesome-infinite,
A peace deep as blessed assurance,
A sense of place
Definitely diminished
By thought
By word.

The Big Ice Reaches The Bay

The big ice sails at night,
Sneaks up the bay from Labrador,
Its bigger floes white battleships
Spaced like the D-Day fleet,
Sitting off the village
Quietly powerful.
A starkly northern armada—
Minesweepers, corvettes, frigates,
P.T. boats, even a Sherman tank
On a landing craft.

In time the wind
Orders it out of the bay
And its recessional is
As quiet as thought.

Smaller vessels straggle,
Remind us that the beautiful
Occupation is only a few miles
Away—on a whim of wind
Will come again.

I'm glad of this:
I like white sinister beauty...
In blue water...
On sunny days...
That never fires a shot in anger.

Inspiration

In winter,
In the basement,
I sift poetic files,
Struggle to shape
Some scraps of inspiration
Into a hard-edged truth.

Gracie the little gray cat
Pads to my office purring,
Jumps on my lap,
Stands on computer keys,
Ascends to the desk,
Sniffs her surroundings,
Declares them perfect,
Settles in for sleep.

Knowing nothing of my angst or aspirations,
She folds her paws under her furry breast,
And effortlessly she becomes a poem.

The Blue Beyond The Golf Green

It came into view on the sixteenth tee
Like something from eternity—
A great blue heron,
Legs extended like a diver's,
Steel-gray wings
A waving blanket of beauty.

The old man addressed his ball,
Waggled his club as though in thrall,
The laughing sphere awaiting the imperfection.
Contact...lift-off...
The shot rose sharply,
Veered left,
Like a space probe gone wrong,
Then dropped to the fairway,
Precipitously, a wounded duck.

"Beautiful," the other said.

Soaring above the tilted world,
Soaring with perfect symmetry,
Soaring into someone else's heart,
The heron landed gracefully
Into the arms of a loving lagoon.

At The Gravesite Of My Ancestor Martell
(1733-1819)

That day in summer we set out early
For the beautifully bleak village
Of Main-a'dieu, where my ancestor settled
After the Louisbourg loss.
Sun brash, sky cloudless,
Sea raised to a glistering blue.

We travelled southeast
Through the wraith-like skeletons
Of evergreen, petrified by fire
Fifteen years before
And burst on sea and the haven of harbour
Ringed by a straggle of houses.

At first we did not find the gravesite
Consumed as it was by buildings
In the heart of the little landfall—
A mere postage-stamp of remembrance,
Fenceless, grass knee-high,
Stones not even standing,
Others daffodil-brocaded faded,
Dates no more than a surmise.

In the center one single tree
Arthritic, alive.

No church, no records, no sail at sea
No laughter and no sorrow,
Only the susurration of the ocean—
Bones, gravestones keeping the rule
Of silence, a whole history
Written upon the cloudless icy blue.
I knelt before these emblems of surcease
Trying to make connection.

Time offered only names...and flowers...
And craggy coast...and blue-black ocean
Welded to the sky.

For Sarah at Seventy-six

I sit here and think of you
In your little apartment on Queen Fredericka,
A senior moored in the big city
Far from the banks of Morien Bay.

I think of all the spunk
Now gone out of you.

A picture still exists of you, a teenager,
A queen on the Homeville bridge,
You hanging out over the bridge
Holding on with one hand,
A fitting symbol for your later life.

Remember the time you came in
The house singing to grandma
The popular song "Who broke the lock
On the outhouse door?" and she so sedate?
It was that kind of spirit that made you.

I remember how you fought our battles,
How you fought your ex to a standstill,
Often beat him up mentally and physically.
How your children raised you and you them,
The way a few brews made you witty
And outgoing and wonderful
When you were, in your later years,
A recluse.

These memories make up a life.

But what is life?
Is it a traffic circle with exits and entrances
And options and traffic jams, too?
What would be the good of it
If it were only a highway
Where you could see for miles ahead
The grain elevators?

Is it a mismatch
Between what we hope for
And what we attain?

You wanted an education,
Yet you had more horse sense
Than a good many university
Professors.

I only know that where the heartbeat is
Age is forever young.
Where the desire is
Age is ageless.
Where the hope is
Age can never conquer.
And where the memory is
Age only wants to wear
Her finest gown.

Therefore, sister,
Consider it an honour
That you have arrived
At a golden age,
Circuitously maybe,
But not at the end of memory.

You may be on borrowed time,
You may have lost some feistiness,
You no doubt have regrets;
But the motor is still running,
The door is open,
And the limousine
Ready for newer jaunts.

Margaree

These naked trees amidst the snow
So moribund, so desolate,
Sleep in a faithful sleep; they know
Their fate:

The snow will knit the broken earth;
Buds will bud often on the limb.
There will be singing at rebirth,
God's hymn.

Lingan: 1983

I saw two crows upon a green
With night-black feathers in a sheen.
One held a worm within its maw;
The other cried with envious "caw."

I saw two of the human race
With Reason, love and will and grace.
One the recipient of a prize,
The other's envy all disguised.

Gowrie School: 1990

Day too warm for late December,
A dream-fog rising from the frozen earth.
The sea solemn as though depressed
By seasonal excess.

I walk the narrow rutted lane—narrower
Than I knew it—past the house where
Lived our Marjorie, telephone operator,
Unofficial historian. On the right
Encroaching alder, mixed with rose bush.
One brazen spruce flounces among the
Brambles. I move around those
Johnny-come-latelies, detect a slab
With steps.

A cement border suggests the dimensions
Of a building: I find the flimsy
Foundation of Gowrie School—gray but
Never dull, solid despite its
Questionable base, its soul indwelling
The village. An impertinent apple tree
Planted by the birds, leans against
The broken steps.

In front a playing field, large when
Eyes knew only largeness, in the days
When we tried to maim each other playing
"pump-pump-pullaway," an indigenous game,
When all the world was Morien. Its
Smallness surprises.

In the village of my memory, I recall
Isabel Gilholm bringing her children
Bananas at recess; Tom Cochrane marching us
Up the lane and down the lane, his barrel
Chest out, his shoulders square, trying
To make soldiers of us for the parade
At the annual fair; the double toilets
Toppling ever so slowly in the black
And happy Halloween night; the school
Inspector pacing the floor, quizzing us

On baseball trivia; the slow and solemn
Ascent up the creaking stairs to see
The principal who carried his strap in
His belt; the laughter of liberation;
The principal's bell cancelling summer.

Gowrie is gone. No memory is the same.
But in our slow forgetting, we can still
Recall our acquiescent days, our dreams
Of moving on, see the coal bin, the
Cloakroom, the central hall, the teacher
At the door, admitting us into prison;
The rowed double desks, anchored in the
Wide-planked room; the pot-bellied stove
With its uneven heat, the picture of
The King and Queen above the teacher's desk;
Pupils scattering like sparrows at the end
Of a busy year; hear the steady drone
Of learning—the little schoolhouse part
Of no global village.

No schooling such as this should be forgotten.

Doves In The Freezing Rain

Doves flew in for breakfast,
I eating bacon and eggs
Brown toast jam tea,
They cracked corn.

One dove landed
Like a jet on a carrier,
All skewed and slapdash.

Unceremoniously, he slid
Into the seed house.

I wore a smile
As broad as Morien Bay.

He caught my twinkle.
Blinked his
Lustrous black eye
In contemptuous
Disapproval.

I must admit
I drank my tea
With unexpected
Pleasure.

Federal Election

Behold the politician
Darting hither and thither
In his black suit,
A gnat on the surface
Of the water.

But I'll take the gnat any day—
Agile, unpretentious, apolitical,
Poetic.

Never drowns in his own lies.
Doesn't have to lie
As he is drowning.
Never has to beg forgiveness
For lying.
Never has to pretend
That he knows your name.

The gnat is a moralist
In a prevaricating world.

For Frances

An old lady now,
All the heartache
Centred in Alzheimer's
Disease.

A washed out face,
Shabby slacks,
An old white sweater,
Riotous hair.
A dying by degrees.

Each day she packs
Unpacks her clothes
For "home."
But where is "home"?

In her drawer
She has four watches
Belonging to other
Patients.

But time means nothing now.

She greets us
In the hall with her coat on
Ready to go "home"—
Greets us as long-lost
Sisters and brothers
Which we are.

We go to the solarium,
Where curiously she has clung
To the hymns she used to know.
Pounds them out on the piano:
"I hear the Saviour calling..."
"Face to face with Christ my Saviour...."
"In times like these ..."

We leave the manor,
Our guilt assuaged,
Knowing she won't remember
We were there.

Christmas Day, 1996

It is Christmas day.
Last night the stores closed early
And all the Santas faded into midnight.
After the mass,
The Saviour was still with us.

It is Christmas day.
A wind blows where it listeth,
Ruffles a royal-blue sea,
King for a King.

I walk in a wood
Spruce-holy—
Mute and adoring.

Unseen warblers
Carol a coming.

The tide,
Like the fulness of time,
Is in.

A festive snows falls,
Whirls in worship.

It is Christmas day—
Earth and sea and sky
A manger.

In Cape Breton

No trains, no local T.V.,
No Air Canada jets,
No free trade, no fish—
Abandonment, exploitation.

But what the heck
We still have the sea,
The harmonious headlands,
The seven-fold amen
Of the land itself,
Saturday night at the local pub,
Tag days at the liquor store,
The grant (much reduced mind you),
Ceilidhs everywhere.

Above all our sense of humour.

The politicians will never
Figure out how to take that
Away from us.

Gulls

Some say gulls are gluttonous,
Will ingest almost anything—
Bones, bread, junk food.
Feed them once you'll have
Freeloaders forever.
They'll squat on your lawn
At dawn, like watchful buddhas.

But when winter's opaque blue makes
Ghosts of them, when wind brushes
Them back as they drift
Above a cliff, creating
Their own art, and when
They blossom behind boats,
Huge white dahlias of the sea,
Then they are poems
With not-so-hidden meanings.

I once found personfication
On a sandbar, a happy gull
Dropping a clam from a height
Onto the hard beige sand,
Going to the heart of the manna.

I saw a lyric at the local wharf,
An immature arctic gull,
Its white wings fringed
By a delicate gray,
Its legs black and spindly,
Its little white head tapered,
Accentuated by a lustrous
Black eye--heavenly symmetry.

Daily, for a week, it performed
The same rhythmic solo,
Soared and circled
And skimmed the surface,
In a weave of beauty,
Oblivious of birders, who
Like magi, came from far,
Because they found such lyricism divine.

Peter Whelan proclaimed the find
In our national newspaper.

Having put the village on the birding map,
The gull, one day, disappeared
Into our imaginations.

And then there was a long ragged tail
Of gulls, poetry in progress,
Returning to the village one evening
At dusk from the local dump,
The fish not swimming here anymore.

All this is to say that I like gulls,
Especially when they laugh and whine
And convocate on chimneys in the cold
And materialize in a hungry flutter.

Then they are found poems.

Because gulls belong to spirit,
And each day, more and more,
I'm tending toward beauty that moves
Truth that is simple
Poetry that I can live by.